EIGHT DAYS A WEEK

Inside The Beatles' Final World Tour

EIGHT DAYS A WEEK

Inside The Beatles' Final World Tour

ROBERT WHITAKER

with Marcus Hearn

METRO BOOKS

NEW YORK

Acknowledgements

The authors are grateful to the staff at Endeavour and Getty Images who made this project possible. In particular we'd like to thank Charles Merullo; production manager Mary Osborne; picture editor Ali Khoja; digital editor Piero Spano and Liz Ihre, who provided transcriptions and proofreading. Thanks also to Richard Reynolds for advice and encouragement.

During our research the following books and magazine proved particularly useful: *The Complete Beatles Chronicle* by Mark Lewisohn; *The Beatles Film and TV Chronicle 1961-1970* by Jorg Pieper and Volker Path; *Mojo*'s *Psychedelic Beatles Special Edition*, edited by Chris Hunt; and, of course, *The Beatles Anthology*.

This 2008 edition published by Metro Books
by arrangement with Endeavour London Limited

Designed by Peri Godbold

Metro Books
122 Fifth Avenue
New York, NY 10011

ISBN-13: 978-1-4351-0950-6

Printed and bound in Singapore

10 9 8 7 6 5 4 3 2 1

Contents

Introduction

1 Germany, 23-27 June

2 Alaska, 27-28 June

3 Japan, 30 June-2 July

4 Hong Kong, 3 July

5 The Philippines, 3-5 July

Introduction

Robert Whitaker in Munich, June 1966.

Brian Epstein framed by peacock feathers, June 1964.

T he pictures in this book are my record of a concert tour that lasted less than two weeks, but which is now regarded as a watershed in the career of The Beatles. They are also the culmination of a journey with the group that had begun over two years before.

I was working at my own studio in Melbourne when The Beatles toured Australia in June 1964. Adrian Rawlings, a journalist friend of mine, suggested that I took some pictures of Brian Epstein, the group's manager, to accompany an article he was writing for *The Jewish News*. There were thousands of fans, and hundreds of journalists, trying to get into the Southern Cross Hotel where The Beatles were staying. However, I don't think anybody had thought of doing an interview with Brian, so Adrian and I beat our way through the crowds and made our way up to his room. Adrian conducted his interview and I started taking some pictures. The room was quite small, and it was impossible to get an angle on Brian which didn't also include the picture frame on the wall behind him. I was concerned that this would ruin the composition of the shot, but I did the best I could. Before we left, Brian told me he would like to see my pictures, so I said I would bring some prints for him the following day.

I got back to my studio and developed the roll of film. Sure enough, the picture frame was a major distraction. As I examined the negatives I noticed that Brian was wearing a gold bracelet and a very expensive watch. Then it dawned on me just what status he had, managing the biggest band to hit Australia, if not the world. Brian was the modern-day equivalent of a Roman emperor, and should therefore be crowned with laurel leaves. I didn't have any laurel leaves to hand, but I did have some peacock feathers, which I laid on top of the photographic paper before I exposed the image. The result was a picture of Brian as a Roman emperor, with the bonus that the feathers covered the offending picture frame.

The next day I put two prints in an envelope and returned to the hotel. The reception desk called Brian and he came downstairs to meet me. As I handed him the envelope the pictures fell onto the floor in front of everybody emerging from the lift. Brian went bright red and suggested we went upstairs.

Brian said he had never seen himself like this and asked me what else I had done. I told him I had an exhibition at the Museum of Modern Art in Melbourne and he said he would take a look. Shortly afterwards I was called back to his hotel and he offered me tickets for The Beatles' performance at Melbourne's Festival Hall. I hadn't heard much by the group before this, and I didn't get to hear much during the concert; my place in the orchestra pit was ten yards away from The Beatles, but it was only five yards away from the screaming kids who drowned out the music.

I met The Beatles and photographed them messing about with boomerangs. Brian then asked me to return to England where his company, NEMS Enterprises, would retain me as a photographer and he would manage me. I was doing pretty well in Melbourne so it took me several months to decide, but I eventually took him up on his offer. Over the next two years I took pictures for album covers by Cilla Black and Gerry and the Pacemakers, and photographed all of Brian's other artists, including Michael Haslam, Billy J Kramer and Tommy Quickly. In-between all of that I would be sent off in various directions to photograph The Beatles.

I was always looking for ways to make the numerous Beatles sessions more interesting. When I was asked to take the pictures that were used on the front of the American album *Beatles '65* I didn't have a clue what to do. We were working at a studio in Farringdon Road, and the people that had been there before had been doing a catalogue shoot. They had left all sorts of bits and pieces behind, such as umbrellas, brooms and a wicker basket. I dreamt up four themed photographs – summer, autumn, winter and spring – using these discarded items as props.

To me a camera is a tool which I can use to record either what I see, or what I dream about. I had seen the film *Un chien andalou*, in which Salvador Dalí and Luis Buñuel recreated and linked a series of dreams. I used this idea as the indirect inspiration for a sequence of Beatles pictures I called 'A Somnambulant Adventure'. I had dreamt about the idolisation of these four boys, and wanted to create a photographic response to that idolisation. The Beatles may have been "bigger than Jesus", to quote John Lennon, but the most famous picture in the Somnambulant Adventure made the point that they were only flesh and blood. It was also an observation that they risked being torn limb from limb by their more obsessive fans. This is the so-called 'Butchers Shot' that was used out of context on the cover of the American album *Yesterday and Today*.

As well as creating pictures for magazines and album covers, I was also asked to take photographs of The Beatles playing live. I first accompanied the group on a cold and damp tour of England where they played cinema stages and clubs, but I was also there when they triumphed at Shea Stadium.

When The Beatles were on tour their time was precious so I never liked asking them to pose in front of museums, statues or other local landmarks. I tried not to get in their way, and they were happy for me to keep taking pictures because I think they realised that every day was different, and each extraordinary event was possibly unique.

With many of their previous tours they had taken the view that they needed to get the job done and get out, but the summer tour of 1966 looked rather more appealing. The Beatles would be returning to Hamburg, where in the early 1960s their residencies in the Reeperbahn clubs had forged their mighty reputation. They were also booked to appear in Japan, an exotic and mysterious country that they had never visited before.

We set off for Germany in June 1966, none of us aware that these would be the last European concerts The Beatles would ever play…

George Harrison with a boomerang given to him by a fan, June 1964.

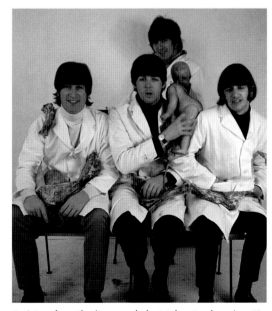

A picture from the 'Somnambulant Adventure' session, March 1966.

1

We always flew first class and the BEA flight to Munich was
no exception. The Beatles had already been around the world at this point – on tour in
America and to the Bahamas to film *Help!* – so this was another day in the office. But it was
quite a good office.

The first leg of the tour was sponsored by the German magazine *Bravo* and we were
accompanied on this part of the journey by Thomas Beyl, one of *Bravo*'s writers. I was there
to take the pictures for *Bravo* and Thomas was there to write the words. Thomas was a
wonderful man and very sympathetic towards The Beatles. He had joined us in London and
presented the group with Bavarian hats and copies of the magazine. He wrote extensively
about the five days he spent with us.

The Beatles arrived at Munich Airport Riem in the early afternoon of Thursday 23 June. Ringo was still wearing his Tyrolean hat when they emerged to face the crowd of fans and reporters that swarmed around the plane.

When The Beatles were on tour it was customary to get a press conference out of the way as soon as they arrived at each destination. The flight to Munich had been relatively brief so this was no problem. These events were organised by Tony Barrow, the group's press officer, and he did his best to marshal the reporters clamouring for answers to their often inane questions. The Beatles had a great knack of responding to these questions with hilarious quips. I think it helped them to get through these sessions, as well as giving the journalists something to write.

As a reportage photographer I was really interested in the way these extraordinary young men interacted with their fans and everyone else who wanted a piece of them. For this photograph I climbed on something to get some perspective on the whole scene in the room.

The first concerts in the 'Bravo-Beatles-Blitztournee' were played at the Circus-Krone-Bau in Marsstrasse, Munich on Friday 24 June. It was a round building used for circus performances throughout the winter, but during the summer the 3,000-seat venue was an ideal location for concerts.

In common with most dates on this tour The Beatles performed twice each day. The afternoon concert at the Circus-Krone-Bau began at 5.15 and the evening one at 9.00. On both occasions the 800-watt Echolette sound system struggled to overcome the audience's frenzied screaming.

I was constantly amazed by the hysteria of The Beatles' fans

and I'm still surprised that humanity could be swayed to such extremes. Several years ago I met Astrid Kerchherr who had photographed the group during their seminal time in Hamburg, and she said, "Imagine what would have happened if any of the boys had actually been caught by one of those fans. They wouldn't have had a stitch of clothing left on!"

It was typically girls who would chase after the group, but occasionally boys would clamber on stage in an effort to make their mark. Every now and then I would look out of the car window and see a charming young lady trying to get the eye of one of The Beatles. More often than not it was only the eye of my camera that caught them.

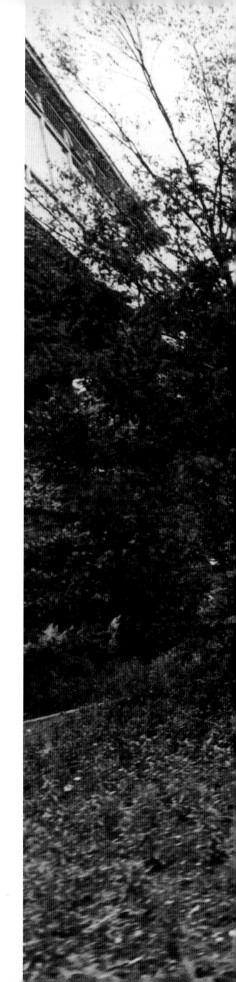

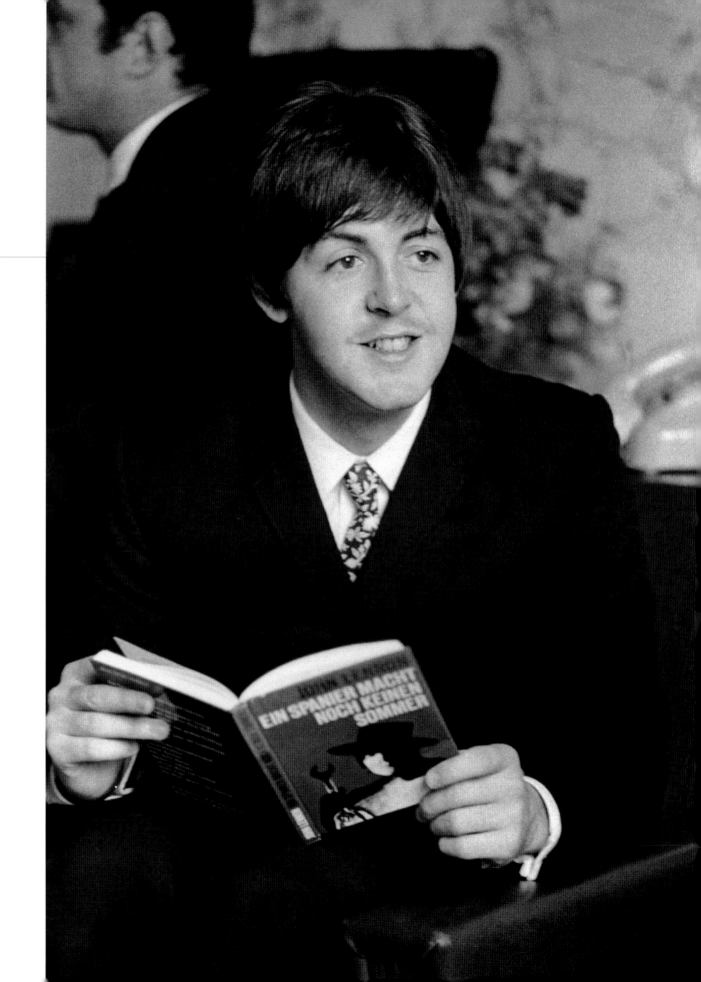

The Beatles stayed at the Hotel Bayerischer Hof in the centre of Munich, one of the finest hotels in Germany. This was typical of the luxury lavished on the group by Bravo magazine. On 24 June the hotel was the venue for a second press conference in-between The Beatles' two performances at the Circus-Krone-Bau.

John's book, *A Spaniard in the Works*, had recently been translated into German and Paul flicked through a copy prior to the second press conference. During the conference our Johnny placed the book prominently on the table in front of the microphones. John and Paul were both incredible songwriters, but in his literary observations on the world John also showed he had a quirky and original sense of humour.

Brian Epstein and Thomas Beyl (far right) preside over the
second press conference in Munich. I had enormous respect for Brian. He wanted The Beatles
to be a first class act and he didn't like them swearing, spitting, or looking like idiots in public.

This press conference gave the editor of *Bravo* magazine the chance to present The Beatles with
'Goldener Bravo-Otto' awards for being the Best Band in the World. The boys were genuinely
honoured but the trophies were quite heavy so they left them behind in Germany. Years later I
visited Thomas Beyl and noticed he still had them in his house.

After the press conference we returned to our rooms upstairs and

Brian was interviewed by Don Short of the *Daily Mirror*. Don (by the standard lamp) was one of the few journalists that The Beatles trusted. All the boys were interested in photography and this wasn't the last time during the tour that Paul would pick up a camera.

Scotch and sickly sweet Coke was The Beatles' favourite

tipple, and the people from *Bravo* magazine understood that it was a requirement in all the hotels we stayed in. As an added bonus they also supplied us with strawberries.

These shots were taken during the relaxed moments after the press conference. George seemed comfortable and his hair was looking great, so I popped these pictures off. As far as I remember, even he liked them.

I didn't get particularly close to George during my time with the group, but I never ceased to find him fascinating. He was thoroughly enjoying his position as a Beatle, but it had struck me that by now he was also looking for something more in his life.

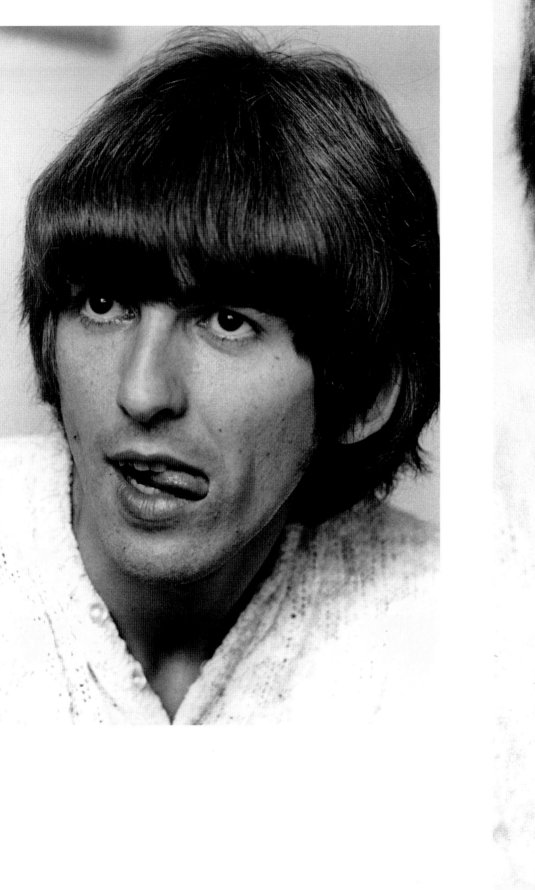

On Saturday 25 June The Beatles boarded a train from Munich for Essen, the next destination on the German leg of the tour. Each Beatle, and each member of their small entourage, was given a suite on the train. George, in particular, remembered being impressed by his marble bathtub.

Our train to Essen had recently been used by the Queen during her visit to West Germany. I remember George saying, "This is how the Royal Family travel and it's rather good."

On Saturday 25 June The Beatles were driven straight from their train to
play the first of two concerts at the Grugahalle in Norbertstrasse, Essen.
There was then time to relax on sun loungers, but by the evening the group
had returned to their dressing room to prepare for another performance.

The Beatles' concerts at the Grugahalle were extremely brief compared to modern shows. The band played for less than half an hour and their repertoire for the German part of the tour comprised just 11 songs. None of these songs were from The Beatles' recently completed, and as yet unnamed, album. This was possibly because they hadn't had the chance to rehearse anything new in the short space of time since finishing work at Abbey Road Studios and flying out to Germany. In fact amateur recordings of the German shows indicate that even when it came to playing familiar tunes such as 'I'm Down' the group were decidedly unsure of themselves.

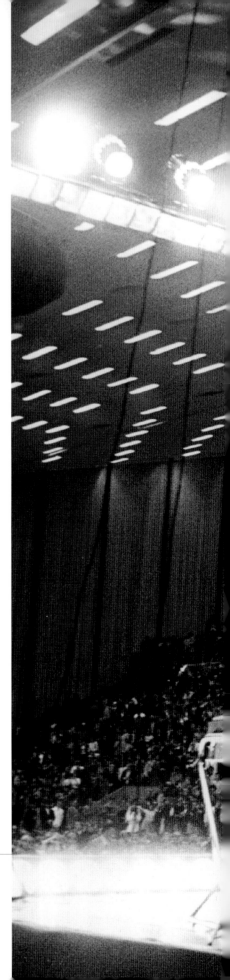

The second Essen show was on the evening of Saturday 25 June. The audiences that day were reportedly rowdier than usual and a number of arrests were made by police following damage to seats and other parts of the Grugahalle.

After the final bow the group were driven straight back to the railway station where they rejoined their train. They arrived at Ahrensburg in Hamburg early in the morning.

Hamburg was a city The Beatles hadn't
visited since the heady days of playing the Star-Club in 1962.
These pictures were taken in the Schloss Hotel and show the
boys experimenting with various forms of new technology – Paul
with a bizarre-looking keyboard and John with the portable tape
recorder which accompanied them for the whole tour.

Neil Aspinall, seen here in the flowery shirt, was the senior road
manager, never far from the group's side. Neil and the other roadie, Mal Evans, did everything for the
boys. There was an extraordinary privacy between Neil, Mal and The Beatles. They had been together
for years and were very tight. The relationship between Brian Epstein and the group was similarly
close. While I travelled with The Beatles I was always aware of the unspoken understanding that I
was not a member of their inner circle.

The Beatles had a strict stage routine that would even extend to what they said between each song. The note taped to the top of George's Epiphone Casino guitar shows the set list for the tour:

'Rock & Roll' ('Rock and Roll Music')
'She's a Woman'
'If I Needed' ('If I Needed Someone')
'Tripper' ('Day Tripper')
'Baby's In Black' ('Baby's In Black')
'I Feel Fine'
'Yesterday'
'Be Your Man' ('I Wanna Be Your Man')
'Nowhere Man'
'Paperback' ('Paperback Writer')
'I'm Down'

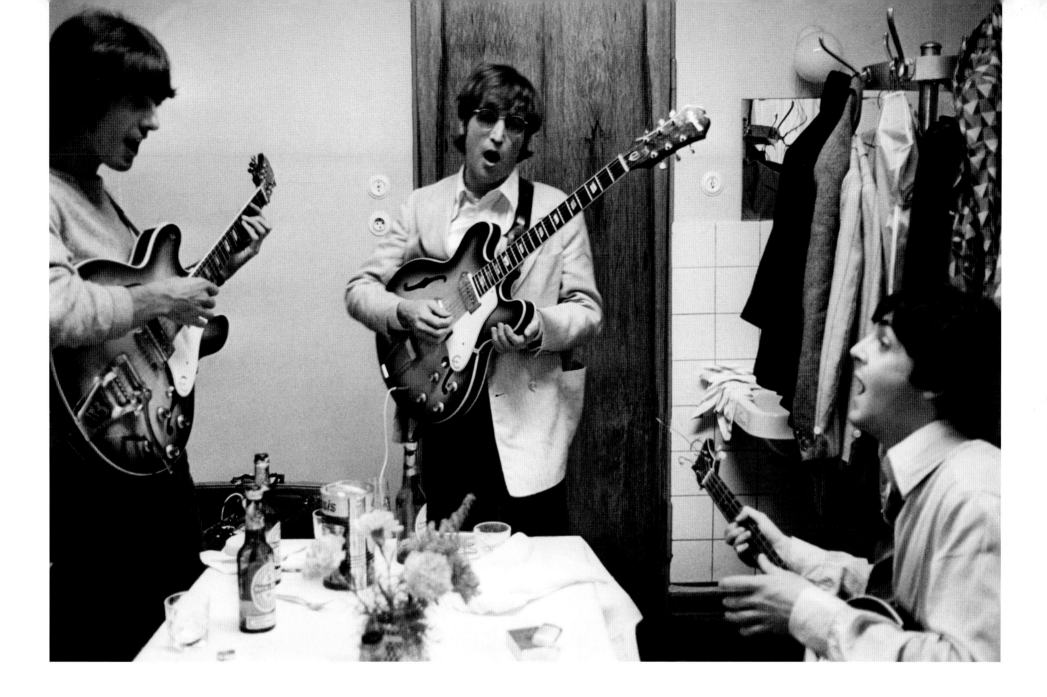

George, John and Paul backstage at the Ernst Merck Halle in
Hamburg, rehearsing to make sure that the presentation of their music would be as good as possible for the
fans. I felt I was there to capture moments like this 'private concert', that this was the sort of relaxed and
revealing shot that the public would prefer to posed pictures and I was very pleased with it.

The final German concerts were played at the Ernst Merck Halle in Jungtusstrasse, Hamburg on Sunday 26 June, to an audience of 5,600 fans.

During their brief visit to Hamburg The Beatles had been reunited with old friends such as photographer Astrid Kerchherr, producer Bert Kaempfert and Star-Club barmaid Bettina Derlien. George, however, remembered encountering some people that he was less pleased to meet. "The bad bit was a lot of ghosts materialised out of the woodwork – people you didn't necessarily want to see again."

Following the second Hamburg performance, a more nostalgic John and Paul rounded off their stay with a midnight visit to the Reeperbahn.

I saw The Beatles perform so many times that I became rather blasé about it. During concerts Neil and Mal would keep a careful eye on the technical and security aspects, while Brian would walk round the back of the stage and out into the audience to watch the group perform.

I was less interested in capturing the group on stage, as I figured there were plenty of other photographers doing that already. For much of the time performance shots were technically difficult anyway: I was so close to the stage that I could rarely get all four of The Beatles in the same shot. I was concerned that if I went too far out into the auditorium I would risk not being able to get back and get left behind.

ALASK

On Monday 27 June The Beatles left Hamburg and flew back to London. Shortly afterwards they boarded another plane to take them to Japan. While they were in the air, however, their pilot received a warning that Typhoon Kit was heading for Japan and he was instructed to make an unscheduled stop in Anchorage, Alaska. Brian Epstein and Tony Barrow were especially concerned about the effect the delay would have on the schedule they had prepared for their arrival in Tokyo but the pilot's prudence was justified: on 28 June Typhoon Kit passed just east of the island of Honshu, where it killed 64 people.

I was only supposed to accompany The Beatles for the German leg of the tour but John said, "It's pointless you staying in London. Why don't you come with us to Tokyo?" I was getting on with them very well by this stage and we were all excited about visiting Japan for the first time. When we arrived back in London I quickly went home to Chiswick to pack a suitcase before I returned to the airport. Alistair Taylor, Brian Epstein's personal assistant, organised the ticket for me but I had to pay the air fare myself.

We were on the way to Japan, flying over the North Pole when we heard we were being diverted to Alaska. We touched down in Anchorage and there was no motorcade to meet us. We crammed into a small bus, with me sitting behind Neil, and drove to a local square box hotel. It was sad to see how the country's natural beauty had been screwed up by these buildings.

Some hasty string-pulling on Brian Epstein's part secured the group an entire floor of the Westwood Hotel for their overnight stay in Anchorage. The Beatles amused themselves by visiting the hotel's top floor club, where their driver Alf Bicknell remembered "we got drunk as skunks". The Beatles were in Anchorage for less than 12 hours but local fans and journalists got to hear about their visit and camped outside the hotel.

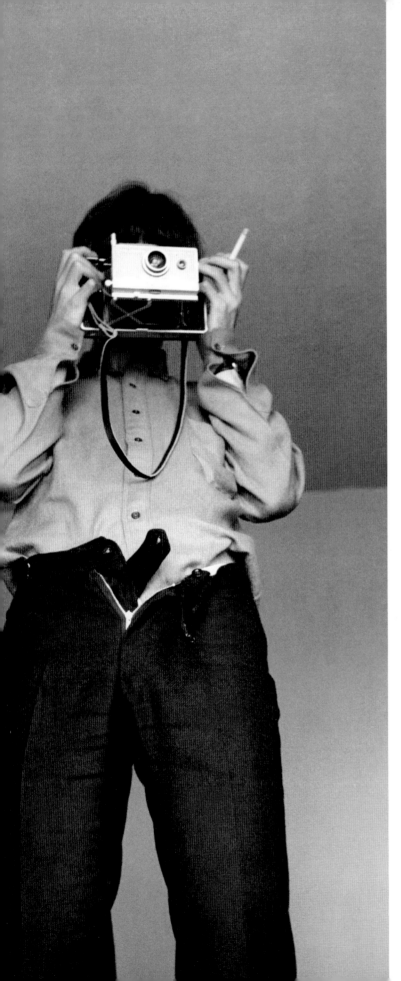

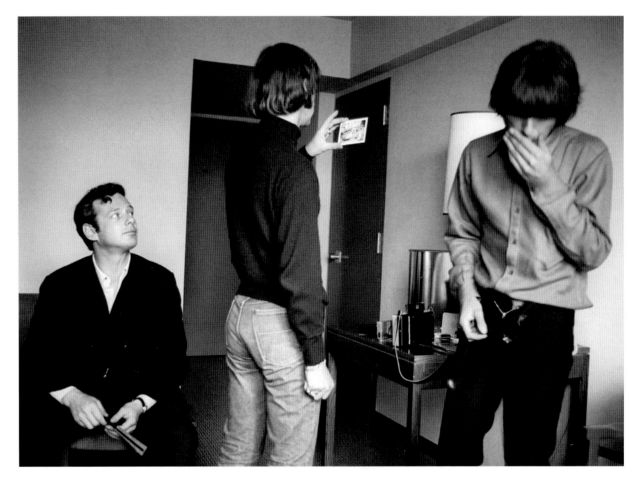

Despite the unscheduled stopover we were still travelling
hopefully and our spirits were high. To relieve the boredom George started messing about with
a Polaroid camera. Brian and John joined him by the window to look at the results. I slipped in
under the three of them and took advantage of the natural light. I think this picture (opposite
page) is a really happy shot of the three of them relaxing.

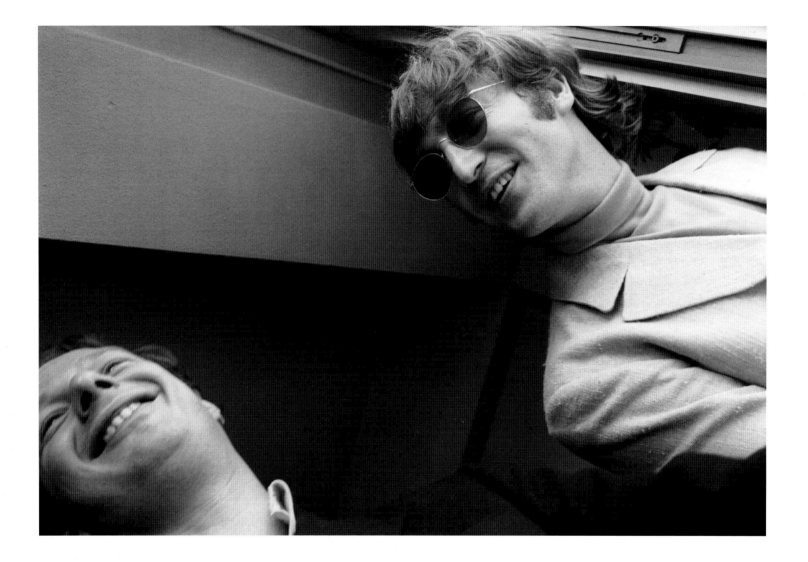

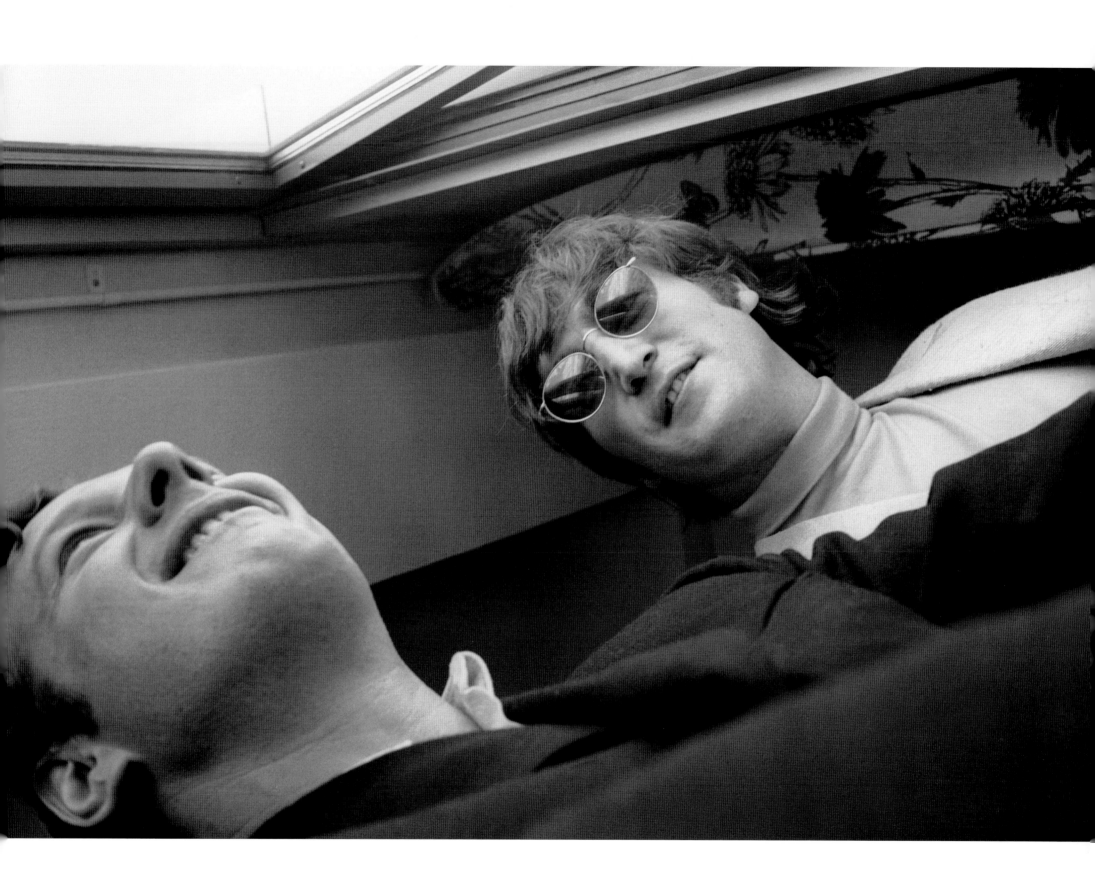

Of all The Beatles I was closest to John. I don't know one
end of a guitar from another so I could never join in when members of the group picked up
their instruments and started jamming – as they did frequently. Instead John and I connected
through a mutual love of surrealism, poetry and painting. Prior to this tour I would visit
John's house in Weybridge and we would paint together. We were both roughly the same age
and we were inquisitive about the world. During quiet moments, such as waiting to leave
Anchorage, we would sometimes have thoughtful conversations.

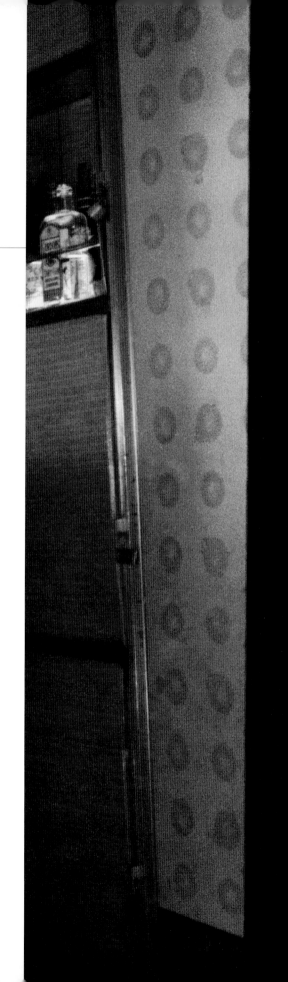

The journey to Japan resumed on Tuesday 28 June.
The band and their entourage donned Japan Airlines'
happi coats while they played cards and taped
conversations on Ringo's portable recorder.

The flight to Tokyo was our first taste of the excellent
treatment we would receive in Japan. The pictures on these pages show an air hostess
attending to Paul, and me deep in conversation with George. This shot was taken by
either John or Paul.

During the flight Ringo played cards with Alf Bicknell
(above left), and dear old Mal Evans. Mal was The Beatles' gofer, and was in charge of
everything from getting their baggage off the plane to making sure their suits were pressed
before a concert. He was the archetypal gentle giant and a really pleasant guy.

The group finally arrived in Japan in the early hours of Wednesday 29 June. It was nearly 4.00am when they stepped off their plane but there were still 1,500 fans waiting to greet them.

We arrived at Haneda Airport to a battery of flash-bulbs and were ushered into Cadillacs for the drive into Tokyo. We were taken straight to the Presidential Suite at the Tokyo Hilton, which is a great hotel. After getting some sleep our first meal boasted various types of Japanese food laid out along this huge dining table. I had smoked a joint before we sat down to eat, and I remember a whole line of waiters arrived carrying tall glasses of iced water. This was their announcement that the meal was about to be served, but to me the clinking ice sounded like a thousand bells ringing in my head.

Security was extremely tight in Tokyo and The Beatles were
effectively confined to their floor of the hotel. They were excited about being in Japan but there
were moments when the time passed slowly. By now I thought they had really grown up as
touring musicians. There were plenty of beautiful geisha on offer, but I remember the boys were
continuously on the phone to their wives and girlfriends back in England.

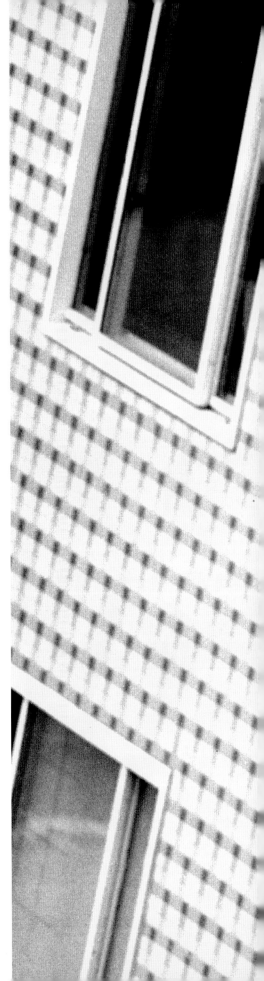

These pictures of John inside the Tokyo Hilton
are amongst those that have not been published before. They're an
interesting illustration of John's darkly mischievous nature, but would
never have been picked up at the time or indeed approved by Brian.

I had arrived in Tokyo with only two rolls of film in my bag but I
soon found myself with another professional assignment. *Life* magazine asked Brian if they could attach a
photographer to the Japanese part of the tour and Brian responded by saying, "We've got one here already!"

Unlike The Beatles, I was free to come and go in Tokyo, although in practice I didn't get much further than
the *Life* office in Ginza, which I visited at the end of each day to deliver film. This was then air-freighted to
New York, where it was developed and printed for that week's edition of the magazine.

This picture shows us leaving the Hilton to head for the Budokan, where The Beatles had been booked to
play a series of concerts. There was a tight security cordon around the hotel which the boys were never fully
aware of. Indeed I don't think any of us were fully aware of the huge police operation that protected the
group's activities.

There had been vociferous protests from those who
considered that the Budokan was a sacred venue that should be exclusively reserved for
martial arts. The Japanese police took these protestors' death threats seriously, and as a result
the fans we saw by the side of the road were herded into small and timid groups. When we
drove to and from the airports in Germany there were throngs of people, but we could go for
long sections of the Japanese roads without seeing a soul. It was all very controlled.

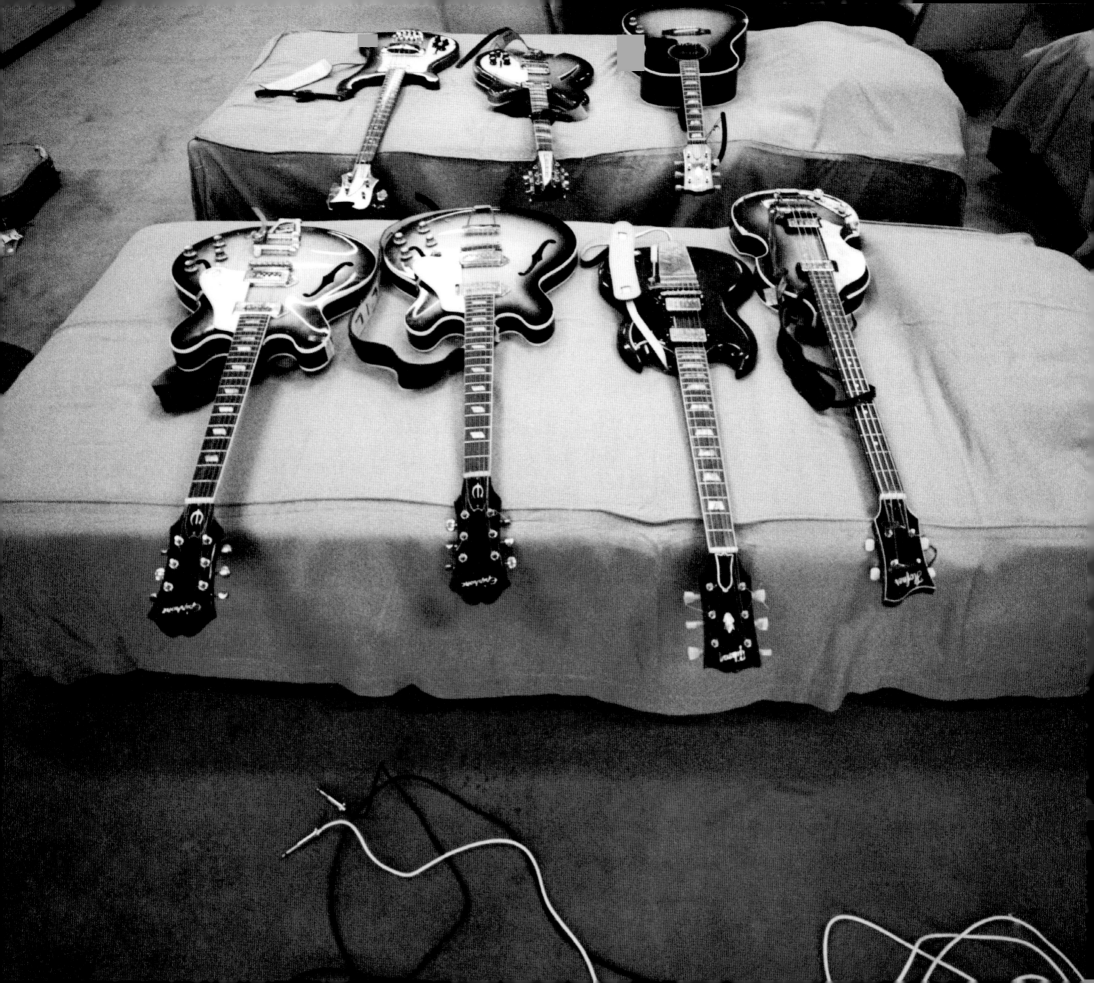

On Thursday 30 June The Beatles played the first of five concerts at the
Nippon Budokan Hall, a huge concrete arena originally built to stage the
judo competition at the 1964 Summer Olympics. The show was video-
taped in colour by the Japanese television company NTV.

The dressing rooms at the Budokan resembled a serene
Japanese painting. The walls were adorned with ceremonial swords, suits of armour
and other valuable antiques in keeping with the building's status as a shrine to the
martial arts. All of us, including The Beatles, were very relaxed. This was the calmest I
had ever seen them before a show, and they were looking forward to it.

I had never seen The Beatles apply make-up before a
performance, but it was necessary for the colour filming. I couldn't resist taking a picture of
George with a powder puff in his hand.

Outside the dressing room, the Budokan was like a mausoleum. The audience was strangely
quiet and there was a heavy police presence on the ground and amongst the fans.

Bob wasn't the only person pointing a camera at the fans
when The Beatles took to the stage at 6.30. Police scanned
the 10,000-strong audience with long telephoto lenses,
looking for potential assassins amongst the crowd.

Whether it was for aesthetic or security reasons, the seats behind the
group were not offered for sale. The Beatles played on a tall stage that
was dressed to look striking on colour television; the name of the group
was picked out in orange and yellow against a vivid blue background.

This picture shows the wayward microphones that prompted Brian Epstein to insist that NTV later shoot another of the group's shows. The Beatles made numerous attempts to secure their faulty microphone stands between and during songs but they never fully succeeded. The result was an awkward and at times bemused performance that Epstein decided was an unfair representation of the band.

It's hard to believe but much of the audience in this enormous venue
heard The Beatles' performance through the relatively small speakers that were usually used to announce
the scores during judo tournaments and other sporting events. I was listening to the group through this PA
system while I was taking pictures. Although the crowd would occasionally scream their general restraint
made it possible to tell that the boys were out of tune, and I remember Neil and Mal commenting on it.

Security was tight both inside and outside the Tokyo Hilton,
with armed police posted in bedrooms, stairwells and lift shafts.
Ignorant of the death threats and other dangers they were facing,
The Beatles delighted in disrupting their captors' incredibly precise
schedules and safety measures.

The Beatles were slightly jealous of the fact that I was able to leave

the hotel on my daily visits to the *Life* magazine office. On my return I would tell them how wonderful Tokyo was and John would ask me about the shops. He told me he had to get out, and once took advantage of the fact that we all looked the same to our guards. He used my name and, accompanied by Neil Aspinall, slipped out of the hotel to visit a local market. It didn't take long before his ruse was discovered and he was brought back to the hotel by anxious police.

The concert promoter, Tatsuji 'Tats' Nagashima, tried to solve the problem by inviting local merchants to the hotel so the boys could buy sunglasses, masks, kites and other souvenirs.

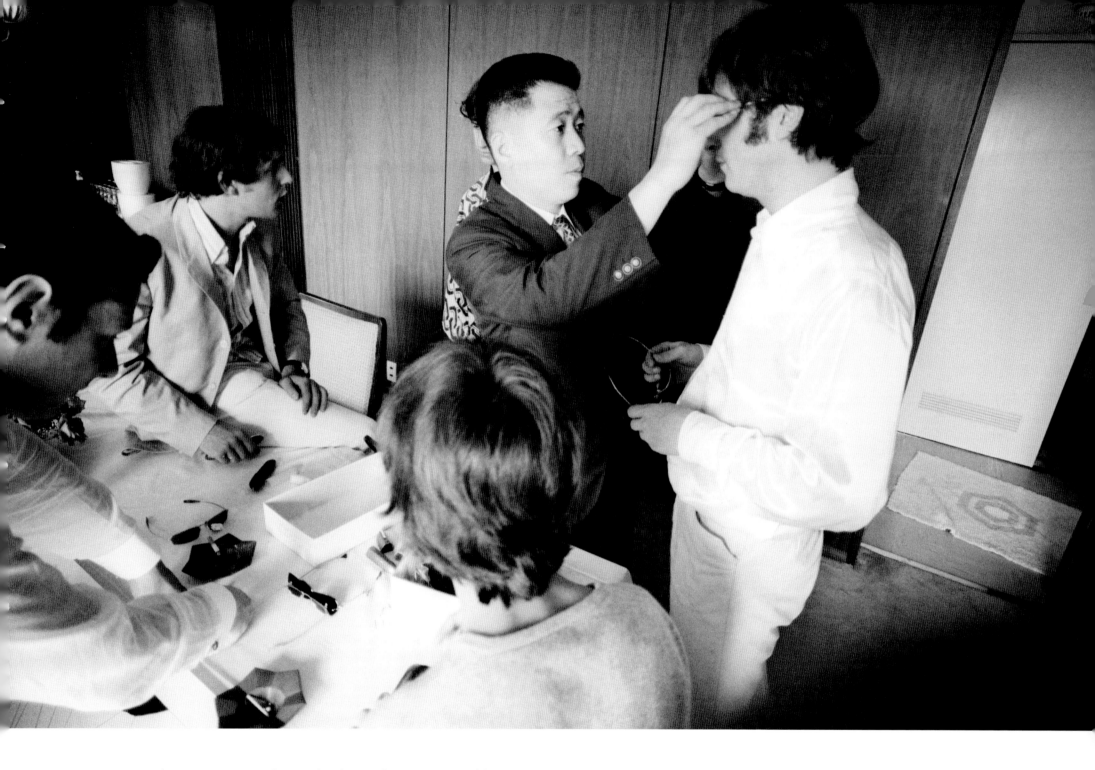

These pictures show the boys being visited by someone selling
sunglasses, and Brian in particular looks very happy and relaxed. Brian changed my life when he asked me to
come and work for him. I owe him a great deal and I've got a lot of fond memories of him.

The pictures over the page show John and Paul messing around with some masks that were brought to the
hotel. John suddenly took one of the masks and shoved it under his jacket, so I took him over to the window
where I had some light and made a picture of him trying to look Japanese.

The group wanted new suits so Tats arranged for the best tailors in
Tokyo to visit the Hilton along with all the other merchants. All the Beatles were very style-conscious and
this picture shows Paul having one of his stage suits measured.

I probably spent less time talking to Paul than any of the other Beatles, but I certainly admired his talent
for writing brilliant music and words. Out of all of them Paul seemed to have the strongest passion for
performing. An enduring memory of him is from one of the group's previous tours in America. He came off
stage after playing Shea Stadium, which must have been an incredible experience, and said "God, I wish we
could have given them more."

Tats was a very generous host and he handed out gifts of cameras
to everyone when we arrived in Japan. I was too broke to buy the best equipment so I was especially
grateful when he offered me some new cameras and lenses.

I used colour film to shoot one of the merchants' visits, partly because I wanted to capture the
colours of the silk robes the boys were being offered. One of the pictures from this session ultimately
appeared on the back of the 1966 compilation album *A Collection of Beatles Oldies*.

One of the lenses Tats gave me transformed
many of the pictures I took on the remainder of the shoot. Up until
this point I had been using very slow Pentax lenses which meant I'd
struggle to hold the camera still under low light conditions. My new
Nikon's metering system and 21mm wide-angle lens meant I could now
take large views of small rooms, with every detail preserved. It was an
absolute revelation.

On Friday 1 July The Beatles played their second and third concerts at the Budokan. The first performance was video-taped in colour by NTV, who later used the material to complement the best songs from the show on 30 June.

The Beatles were aware that they had been out of tune during their first concert at the Budokan. They didn't take this sort of thing lightly, so prior to the show on 1 July there was a lengthy rehearsal in their spacious dressing room. Here were four guys who were genuinely trying to give a great performance. They realised something was wrong so they tried to put it right.

The Nikon 21mm lens came with a little viewfinder. As soon as I looked through it I thought, "Here's my new world." Everywhere I looked I saw the most amazing images. For these shots in the Budokan dressing room I lay on the ground and looked up, experimenting with the lens as The Beatles rehearsed.

This sequence showing The Beatles leaving their dressing
room and heading for the Budokan stage (accompanied, as ever, by numerous policemen)
conveys the building excitement as they get closer to the audience. I didn't always look
through the viewfinder, and the picture opposite was literally shot from the hip.

The Beatles played the same 11 songs on 1 July as they had on 30 June, but their performance was more polished. The NTV recording of the first show on this day reveals Paul's obvious delight that on this occasion his microphone is going to stay put.

Although The Beatles didn't play any songs from their new album on this tour they did perform 'Paperback Writer' (which days before had reached Number 1 in the UK and US) and their forthcoming single 'Nowhere Man'. Both songs required a cappella introductions which the group sometimes struggled to reproduce.

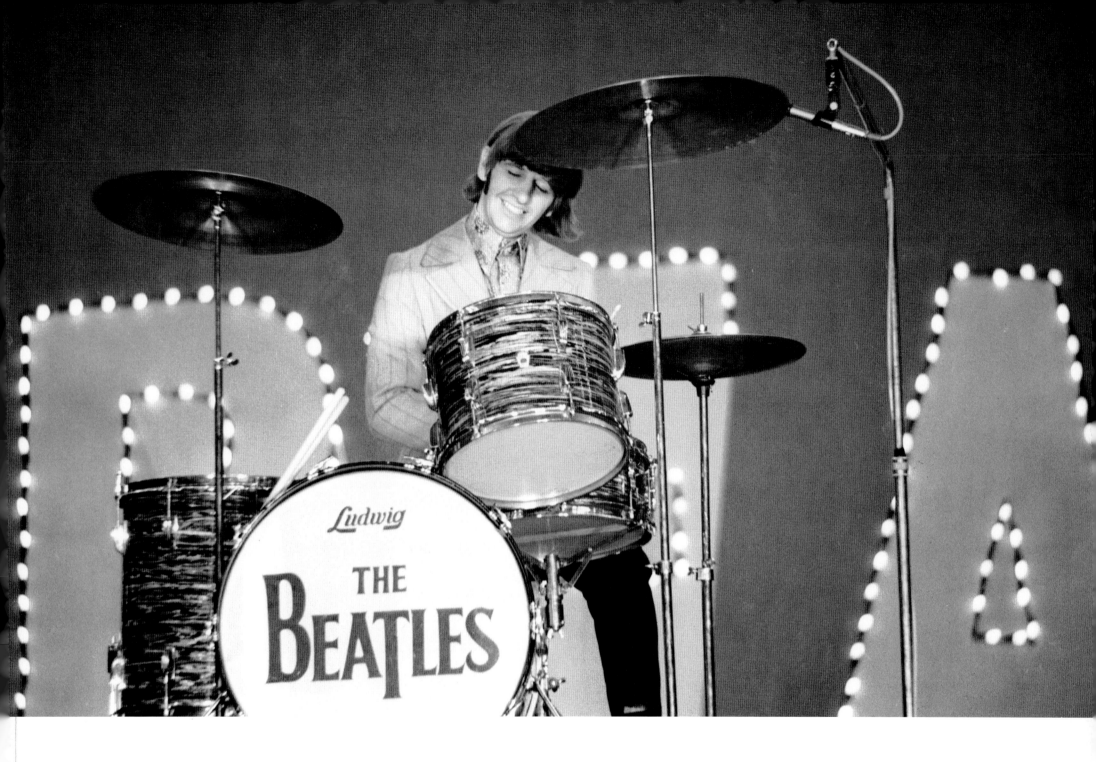

I don't know whether it was to preserve the wooden floor of the Budokan, or whether it was intended as a security measure to prevent anyone jumping up, but The Beatles played on an elevated stage that was about eight feet off the ground. Ringo sat on a podium on top of that stage so he was even higher than the others.

Back at the hotel between concerts I think it was sheer
boredom that prompted The Beatles to begin painting. John, or possibly Paul, asked Tats to
supply them with paint and some beautiful Japanese paper. Over the course of two nights The
Beatles collaborated on their only joint venture that didn't involve music. They placed the
paper on a small table and put a lamp in the middle. Each of them took a corner of the paper
and started painting towards the light. John and Paul used heavy acrylics, while Ringo – and
I think George – used watercolours. They never discussed what they were painting. The end
result, and how it all joined up, evolved naturally.

I used my new camera and lens to photograph their progress, illuminated only by the lamp's
60 watt bulb. An acetate of the new Beatles album had recently arrived from London and we
listened to it over and over again while they were painting. They decided to name the album
Revolver, and it played continuously in the background while they debated the running
order of the songs and wondered if there was anything they could have done differently. I felt
privileged to be among the first to hear this incredible music in the company of the guys who
had created it.

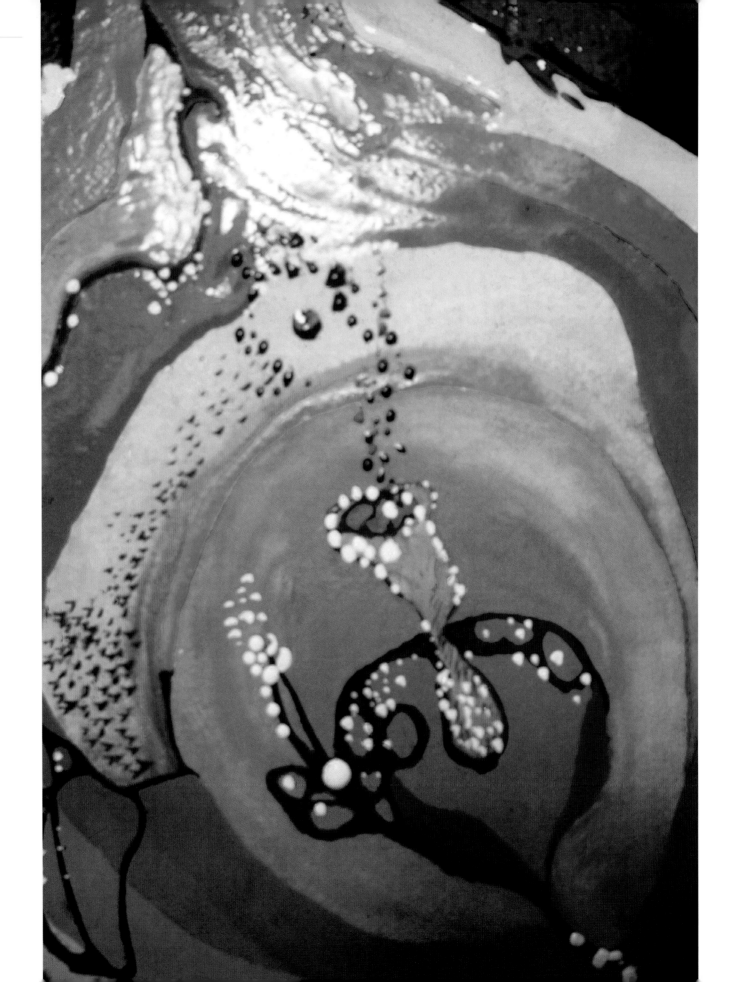

ビートルズの4人が、1枚のキャンバスに寄せ書きした絵で、当時、ファン・クラブ会長だった下山鉄三郎氏に、ビートルズ自身から手渡されたもの。

The Beatles' completed painting is now informally known as 'Images of a Woman'. Tats Nagashima suggested that the painting should be sold for charity, and it was purchased by cinema manager and fan club president Tetsusaburo Shimoyama. In the mid-1990s the painting was reportedly sold to a dealer in Osaka for ¥15 million.

In 2002 the painting changed hands again, when the Internet auction site eBay offered it for sale. In May that year the Liverpool Echo reported that the painting was expected to sell for over £350,000 and quoted an eBay spokesman:"We certainly believe this picture is as great as Picasso's and Van Gogh's, although the quality is completely different. And it is not too much to regard 'Images of a Woman' as the one and only Beatles' painted picture in the world."

The group left the Hilton to play their final two concerts at the Budokan on Saturday 2 July. Despite the protests over The Beatles' performances there had been around 209,000 applications for the first 30,000 tickets that were made available, and now all 50,000 tickets had been sold by means of a lottery system.

A report on The Beatles' visit was sent to the Foreign Office by Dudley Cheke, a chargé d'affaires at the British Embassy. Cheke claimed that The Beatles had "swept the youth of Japan off their feet. In sober truth, no recent event connected with the UK has made a comparable impact in Tokyo – a 'Beatles mood' has gripped this city."

Before they unpacked their light grey, pinstriped suits, The Beatles once again went through a meticulous rehearsal before their final concerts at the Budokan.

On days when The Beatles

were playing live Mal would go ahead of the
group and set up their amplifiers and other
equipment on stage. Once everything was
ready he would join the group backstage
and help them with their guitars. He was an
indispensable member of the team and was
in his element during these tours.

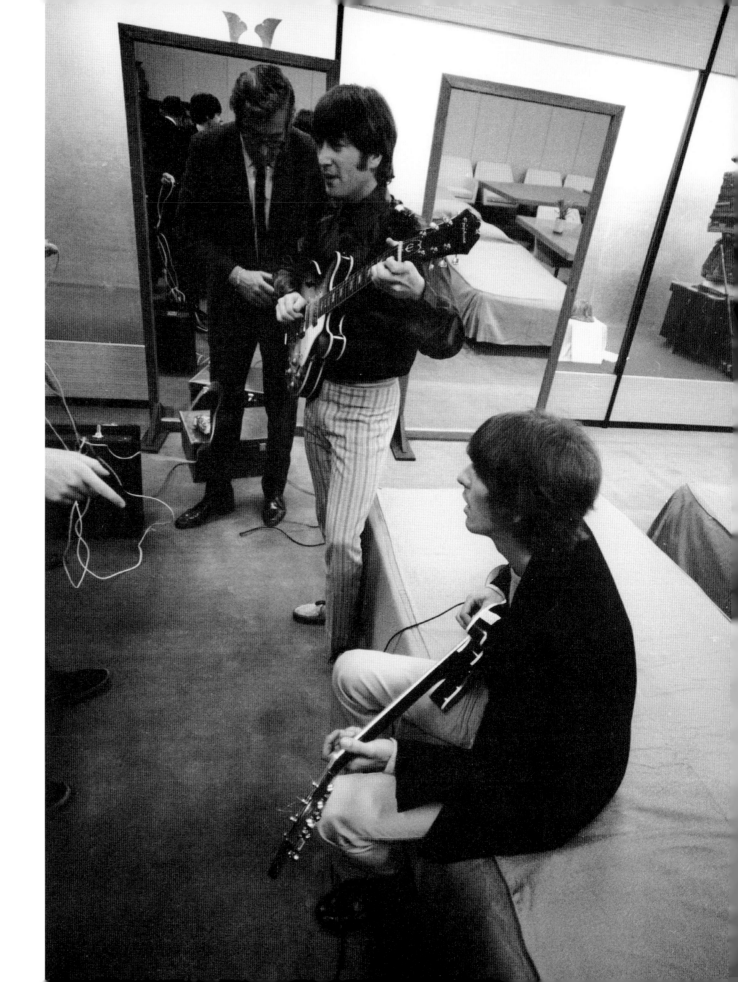

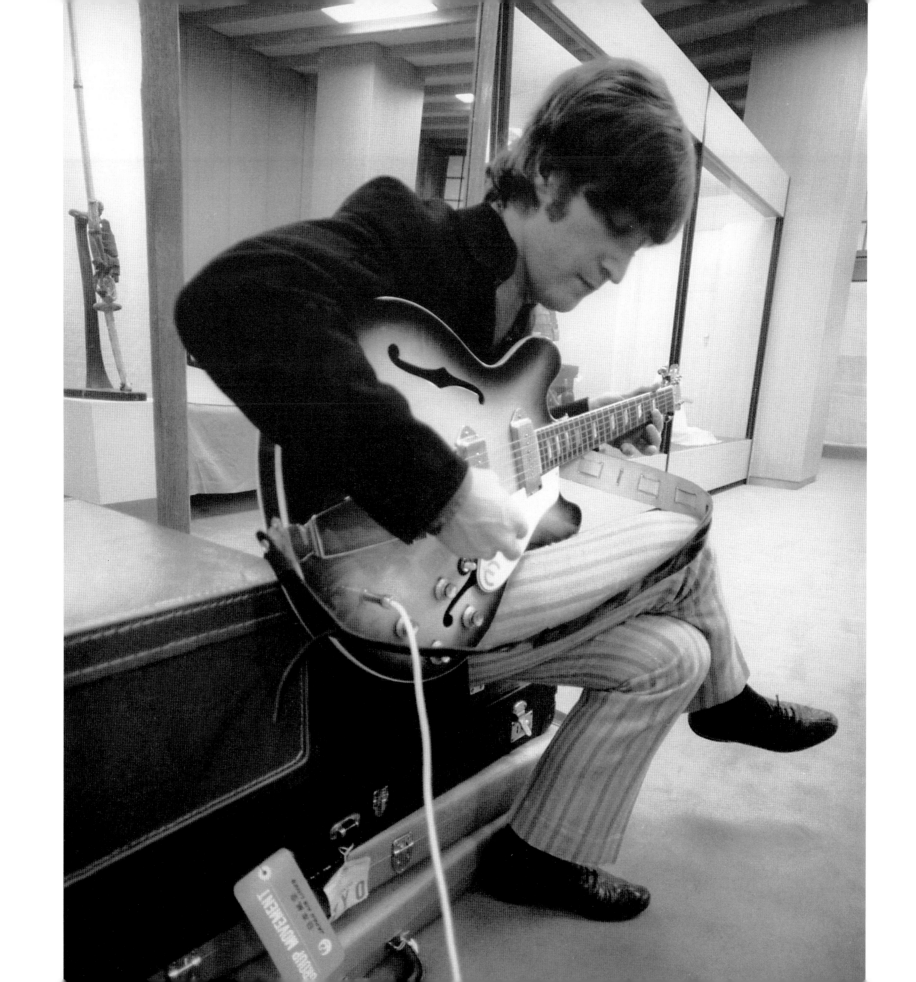

The Beatles had come to Japan to sell a lot of records and entertain a lot of people, and they had done both of those things. Perhaps understandably Brian hadn't told them the whole story about the security threats, but they seemed to brush aside whatever concerns they may have had. Despite the protests of a vocal minority they knew that the fans had wanted them there and the Budokan had wanted them there.

Japan had been a pleasant surprise to all of us, and I felt
I hadn't scratched the surface of the country during our brief visit. The hotel was great,
the Budokan was wonderful and even the dressing rooms had been impressive. Every
element of The Beatles' schedule had been planned in minute detail and it had been a
very smooth operation.

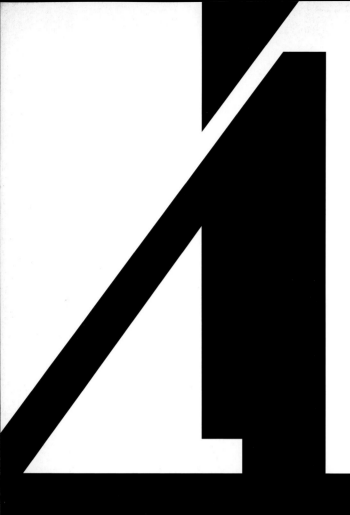

HONG KONG, 3 July

The final concerts of The Beatles' summer tour were due to be played in Manila, the capital of the Philippines. The flight from Tokyo to Hong Kong, where they were due to change planes for Manila, left on the morning of Sunday 3 July.

The Beatles had different ways to amuse themselves during long journeys. They would read, play games or mess about with Ringo's tape recorder. When John wasn't buried in a book he would often write or doodle. This time I was intrigued by what he was drawing. I looked over his shoulder and to my amusement he was defacing a picture of the group.

In late morning, The Beatles' Japan Airlines plane landed in Hong Kong where there was a 70-minute delay until the group boarded the connecting flight to Manila.

In Hong Kong, and indeed most places we had been, there

was always a hubbub to greet us. The picture above of Kaitak Airport shows the fans in the distance, waiting to catch a glimpse of the band. The picture opposite shows what looks like a peculiar stand-off as press photographers gather round the group.

These pictures were taken in the airport's VIP lounge, where
journalists had waited to conduct pre-arranged interviews.

I was always interested in capturing the intensity of the interest in the group, which often
extended to Brian Epstein. The boys and Brian would try to answer as diligently as they could
in the short time available. Within an hour we were back on the tarmac outside, ready to
board our plane.

Before we left Hong Kong some of the air
hostesses from Cathay Pacific, with whom we were flying to Manila,
handed out gifts of flowers which, needless to say, pleased John, Paul,
George and Ringo. We had been treated respectfully by our hosts in
every country we had visited. At our next destination, however, all that
was about to change…

THE PHIL

Aboard the flight to Manila the group discussed their plans for their two-day stay in the Philippines with Brian and Alf Bicknell. They were accompanied on the journey by Vic Lewis, the NEMS executive who had booked The Beatles' forthcoming concerts with local promoter Ramon Ramos. Epstein and Lewis didn't think to mention that they had declined a request from Ramos for The Beatles to attend a lunch hosted by Imelda Marcos. The Beatles had been invited to visit the first lady at Malacañang Palace at 11.00am the following morning, and the Manila Sunday Times had already reported that the group would be attending.

1966 saw the beginning of what became known as 'Flower Power', and this new trend was reflected in the psychedelic shirts The Beatles had started to wear. Ringo's paisley creation came from a shop called Hung On You, which was run by Michael Rainey. Hung On You was in Chelsea and was the forerunner of Biba, but on a much grander scale. The Beatles also bought a lot of clothes at the Dandy Boutique, which was run by John Crittle. Michael and John were pioneers of the 'tune in, turn on, drop out' fashions that would soon become the predominant look for young people.

On arriving in Manila The Beatles were shown into a white limousine and driven away before the rest of their party knew what was happening or even where they were going. It was common for the four Beatles to bypass airport procedures when landing in a country, but in this instance it had happened so quickly that they had become separated from the hand luggage containing their marijuana. Fearing that the drugs would be discovered by the airport authorities, Neil Aspinall grabbed the cases and gave chase in another car. Brian Epstein eventually caught up with the group aboard a luxury yacht owned by local millionaire Manolo Elizalde. The Beatles' visit to the yacht had been arranged by Ramon Ramos, possibly as a favour to Elizalde's son, Manuel. Furious about the way the group had been hijacked without his permission, Epstein demanded they were taken to their hotel immediately.

I remember feeling uncomfortable as soon as we arrived in Manila. The Beatles were immediately separated from the rest of us and whisked away with their bags still on the runway. The rest of us headed for our hotel, where the boys eventually joined us at 4.00am.

On Monday 4 July two men arrived to escort The Beatles to their appointment with Imelda Marcos, but Epstein *refused to wake them up. Later that morning Paul and Neil sneaked out of their hotel. Paul bought some souvenir paintings in the shanty town adjoining Manila's financial district and then drove to some sand dunes for a discreet smoke. They arrived back to see hysterical live TV coverage of The Beatles' non-appearance at the presidential palace. Ramon Ramos tried to diffuse the situation and asked The Beatles to visit the palace, but the group generally made it a rule to decline such official invitations and, in addition, they were due on stage at 4 o'clock. They stood their ground and ignored Ramos's suggestion in order to relax and prepare for the show.*

We spent the afternoon huddled in the stadium's dressing room, which was much smaller than The Beatles were used to and quite a comedown after the Budokan. The stadium itself resembled a second-hand prison camp and I was already starting to regard the whole experience as a real downer.

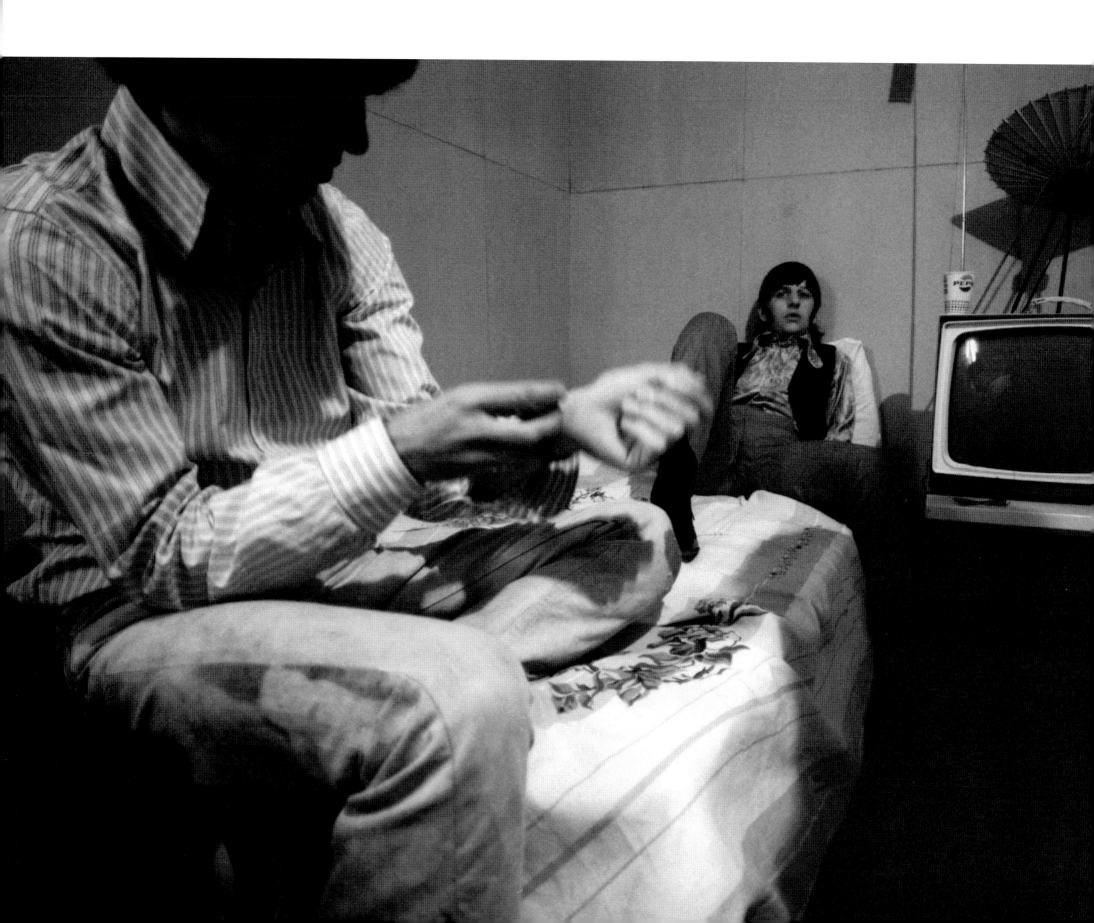

These pictures illustrate the
cramped conditions backstage, but what they don't
show is the incredible humidity we had to endure.
We were unaware of how serious the Imelda Marcos
situation was about to become, but there was
already an air of anxiety because of the conditions
and the strange way we had been treated.

There was a heavy police presence, just as there had been in Japan,
but in Manila the audience was separated from the stage by tall wire fences. There were enormous crowds
for both the concerts The Beatles played on that day, but several things caught my eye prior to the first show.
The first was a Western girl staring wistfully out from a sea of Asian faces. I was also intrigued by an area
that was presumably reserved for dignitaries who didn't seem to have turned up. It was strange to see a block
of empty seats when elsewhere the audience was packed in so tightly.

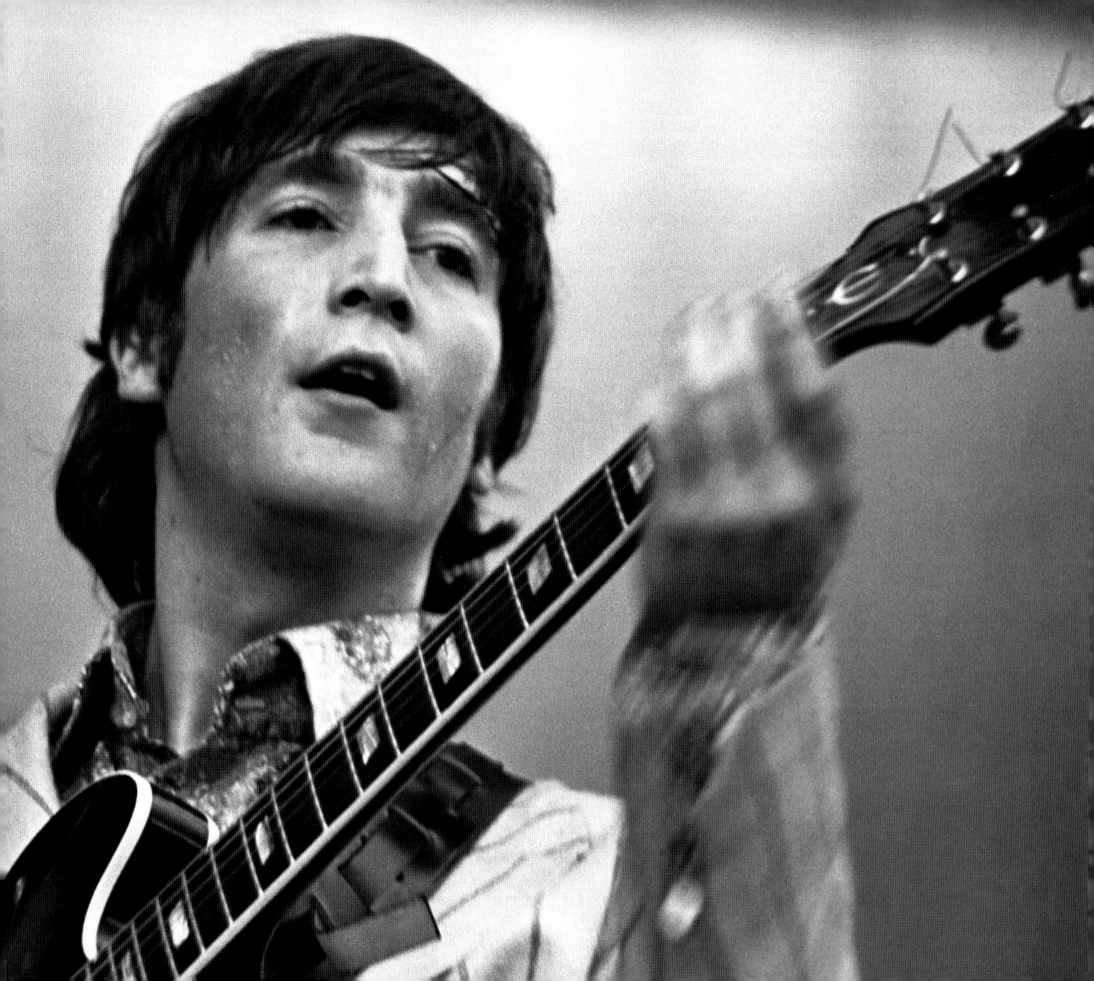

On Monday 4 July The Beatles played two shows at the Rizal Stadium. In the afternoon they played to over 30,000 fans and in the evening to over 50,000. There were suspicions in the Beatles camp that the second show in particular had been oversold. The combined audience for the two Manila shows was the largest number of people The Beatles played to in their entire career.

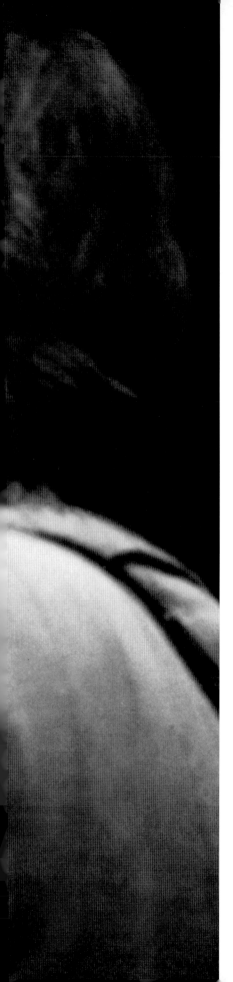

I had a clear view of the group and used the opportunity to take some
closer-than-usual shots of them in performance. They hadn't been on stage for very long when the humidity
started to get to them. Some of these pictures clearly show the sweat pouring off.

I got on very well with Ringo, who's a wonderful guy and one of the
most humorous people I've ever met. I liked the way he could diffuse an awkward situation with a well-timed
quip, and I also admired his dress sense. From the red-striped suit he wore in Germany to the paisley Hung
On You shirt he wore when we arrived in Manila he always looked very stylish.

Tired and jetlagged, The Beatles returned to their hotel after the second show. They awoke on the morning of Tuesday 5 July to discover that the Manila newspapers had described their failure to visit Mrs Marcos as a deliberate snub. The Manila authorities, who seemed to take an instant dislike to The Beatles on their arrival, now turned distinctly hostile. The hotel food either didn't appear or was inedible, and the group's police protection virtually disappeared. Brian Epstein and Tony Barrow hastily organised a televised press conference to clarify their position, but Brian's explanation was rendered unintelligible by a mysterious technical fault that lasted throughout his speech. Amidst growing fears for The Beatles' safety it was decided to beat a hasty retreat to the airport. The group arrived to find an angry crowd chanting "Beatles alis dayan!" – "Beatles go home!"

Mal packed our souvenirs before we took the bags, instruments and amplifiers to the airport. There was no police escort, so we felt we were at the mercy of the ugly crowd. As Alf and I were driven to the airport, there was a guy next to our driver who pointed a gun at us. He was pretty rough.

Brian, Mal and Alf were all knocked about in scuffles that took place at the airport. Concerned for their own safety, John and Ringo hid behind a group of nuns, whilst George took shelter behind some Buddhist monks.

There were no privileges at the airport, so the boys had to carry their own bags. We had to fight our way through the crowds to get to the check-in desk and then to get to the departure lounge. I remember Ringo had an alabaster chess set which was knocked out of his hands. We felt lucky to get on the plane, but then we were held on the runway for what seemed like ages. Brian was taken off the plane and made to hand over a special 'tax' before we were allowed to take off. It was huge relief to get out of that hell-hole.

The plane finally took off at 4.45pm. The Beatles had escaped unharmed, but without any payment for their concerts. John vowed to "never go to any nut-houses again", and George told the press that an atom bomb should be dropped on Manila. Years later, when Alf Bicknell recounted his experiences with The Beatles as an after dinner-speaker, he asked George for an endorsement. George came up with, "Anyone who was beaten up by Imelda Marcos's bully squad is a friend of mine."

The Beatles were disturbed by the numerous threats to their safety and frustrated by the fact that neither they, nor their audience, could hear what they were playing. A game of cards helped to calm our nerves, but I think the incident in Manila strengthened their resolve to stop playing live. And with the end of the tour came the end of my long association with the group.

After the concerts in the Philippines The Beatles went to

New Delhi and I went to Athens for a holiday of my own. In August 1966 The Beatles fulfilled an obligation to play some dates in America and then quietly retired from touring.

Brian and I ended our arrangement on perfectly amicable terms and I moved on to other projects. In 1967 I worked with my friend Martin Sharp on the cover of the Cream album *Disraeli Gears*. That same year I joined Martin in establishing the English edition of the satirical magazine *Oz*.

I was reunited with The Beatles at the opening of the Apple shop in Baker Street but I never saw George or Paul after that. John was a good friend, however, and we stayed in touch for years. He would call me from America and ask me when I was coming out to New York. I also stayed in touch with John's wife, Cynthia, and I thought it was a great shame when they split up.

In 1968 I married Susan and started moving away from music photography. My career took me to the Vietnam War, where I was badly wounded, and collaborations with such diverse characters as Mick Jagger and Salvador Dalí. In December 1970 I covered the Indo-Pakistani War for *The Observer* and was jailed for espionage. But all of that is another story.

In the 1970s Susan and I became farmers, and I put my entire archive of negatives into tea chests which I stored in the chicken shed. Most of those negatives have stayed in those tea chests until now.

It's possible that my photographs of The Beatles have overshadowed my other work, and if that's the case I'm happy to live with it. Part of me is surprised that people should still want to look at these pictures over 40 years later, but I'm also aware that interest in John, Paul, George and Ringo has never diminished.

Let the last words be from one of them. About five years ago I was in Chelsea when I bumped into Ringo. We greeted each other warmly but Ringo's wife, Barbara, looked confused. "This is Bobby," he explained, smiling. "He took some pictures of us in the 60s."